LIGHTHOUSES

MAN-MADE WONDERS

Jason Cooper

Rourke Enterprises, Inc.
Vero Beach, Florida 32964

PHOTO CREDITS

© Lynn M. Stone: cover, pages 4, 7, 10, 12, 15, 18, 21;
© James P. Rowan: pages 8, 13, 17; © Jerry Hennen: title page

LIBRARY OF CONGRESS
Library of Congress Cataloging-in-Publication Data
Cooper, Jason, 1942-
   Lighthouses / by Jason Cooper.
   p. cm. — (Man made wonders)
   Includes index.
   Summary: An introduction to lighthouses, their history,
keepers, and use.
   ISBN 0-86592-630-1
   1. Lighthouses—Juvenile literature. [1. Lighthouses.]
I. Title. II. Series.
VK1013.C66 1991
387.1'55—dc20   91-12277
                  CIP
                  AC

TABLE OF CONTENTS

LIGHTHOUSES

Here and there along the world's seashores are lighthouses. Lighthouses send powerful beams of light into the night.

What we call a lighthouse may be a tower, building, or platform. Each kind of lighthouse has its light pointed toward the sea or a great lake.

A lighthouse warns ships that land and perhaps rocks or shallow water are nearby.

Sea captains identify a lighthouse by the way its light flashes. The lighthouse helps a captain learn the ship's exact location.

ghthouse at Provincetown, Massachusetts

KINDS OF LIGHTHOUSES

Lighthouses may look like silos, tubes, or chimneys with glass tops. One type of lighthouse looks like a house on stilts. Its light is on the roof.

Another type of lighthouse has its light on the top of a tall skeleton of steel beams.

Many lighthouses are white. But striped or checkered lighthouses are not unusual. The shape and color of a lighthouse help identify it in daylight.

Steel frame lighthouse
Sanibel Island, Florida

EARLY LIGHTHOUSES

People on land have used lights to guide sailors for thousands of years. The first lighthouses, however, were not buildings. They were simply fires lit on high ground so that ships could see them. Later, fires to warn ships were built on stone towers.

The tallest lighthouse in history was built almost 2,300 years ago by the Egyptians. It stood over 400 feet tall. An open fire burning on top was its light.

Roman-built lighthouse from 1,800 years ago and church in Dover, England

MODERN LIGHTHOUSES

For hundreds of years, lighthouses were important to sailors. In the early 1900s there were still about 1,500 **operating** lighthouses in the United States alone.

Today, fewer than 500 lighthouses in the United States and Canada still operate their lights.

A lighthouse's main purpose is to help a ship find its way. Radio signals are more important to ships now than guiding lights. Radio signals are often sent from lighthouses.

eceta Head Lighthouse, built in 1894, on Oregon coast

Lighthouse on stilts at Gasparilla Island, Florida

Lighthouse in Two Harbors, Minnesota, on Lake Superior

THE LIGHTHOUSE BEACON

Over the **centuries,** lighthouses have been powered by fire, kerosene, gasoline, animal fat, oil, and other fuels. Today's lighthouses operate on electricity.

The beam, or **beacon,** of light that a lighthouse sends may be seen over twenty miles at sea. Foggy weather, of course, limits the distance.

A lighthouse beacon shines through special glass to make the light brighter. The shape of the glass and the speed at which the light flashes help make each lighthouse beacon different.

14

Modern lighthouse beacons are powered by electricity

HOW A LIGHTHOUSE WORKS

A lighthouse may flash a white, red, or green beam of light. It may also flash a mix of colors.

Ship captains have guides to lighthouses. The captain can identify the lighthouse and its location by the color and timing of the light flashes.

Lighthouse beacons are not very helpful in fog. Ships in fog listen to a lighthouse's sounds—foghorns, sirens, bells, and radio signals.

Head Lighthouse in Bass Harbor, Main

BUILDING A LIGHTHOUSE

Lighthouses are built where their light can be seen for many miles. Some are built close to sea level. Others stand on great **headlands,** high points of land that stand in the sea.

Lighthouses have to withstand wind and storms. Those closest to the water are built to stand up to waves, too.

Lighthouses may be made of wood, brick, stone, concrete, or steel. Where a lighthouse will be built helps to decide what materials will be used to build it.

*⊃ceta Head Lighthouse on
foggy Oregon coast*

LIGHTHOUSE OWNERS

Lighthouses in the United States still in use are under control of the United States Coast Guard. Canada's lighthouses are operated by the Department of Transport.

What most people call a lighthouse, the Coast Guard may call a "light station." The Coast Guard's "lighthouses" operate with part-time workers. "Light stations" are run by full-time workers.

20 *U.S. Coast Guard operates America*
lighthouses, including this one
at Old Saybrook, Connecticut

INDEX

Glossary

beacon (BEE kun) — a light used as a signal; a narrow beam of light

century (SENCH er ee) — a period of 100 years

headland (HED land) — a high point of land jutting into the sea

keeper (KEE per) — the person who operates a lighthouse

operating (AH per a ting) — working as it is supposed to; still being used

KEEPERS OF THE LIGHT

Like railroad crossing gates, many lighthouses work without anybody having to be there. Some lighthouses, however, have a **keeper.** A keeper is the person who runs a lighthouse.

The keeper watches for changes in weather, turns on fog signals, and takes care of equipment.

A lighthouse keeper lives in buildings near the lighthouse. A keeper may be in the Coast Guard or someone hired by the Coast Guard.

Once upon a time, before electricity, all lighthouses had keepers. They often lived in cold, lonesome surroundings.